AF093627

THE POETRY OF THORIUM

The Poetry of Thorium

Walter the Educator

Silent King Books

SILENT KING BOOKS

SKB

Copyright © 2024 by Walter the Educator

All rights reserved. No part of this book may be reproduced in any manner whatsoever without written permission except in the case of brief quotations embodied in critical articles and reviews.

First Printing, 2024

Disclaimer
This book is a literary work; poems are not about specific persons, locations, situations, and/or circumstances unless mentioned in a historical context. This book is for entertainment and informational purposes only. The author and publisher offer this information without warranties expressed or implied. No matter the grounds, neither the author nor the publisher will be accountable for any losses, injuries, or other damages caused by the reader's use of this book. The use of this book acknowledges an understanding and acceptance of this disclaimer.

"Earning a degree in chemistry changed my life!"
- Walter the Educator

dedicated to all the chemistry lovers, like myself, across the world

THORIUM

In the heart of stars, where fusion ignites,

THORIUM

Resides a metal, a silent might,

THORIUM

Thorium, its name, with atomic grace,

THORIUM

In the cosmic dance, it finds its place.

THORIUM

A quiet guardian of Earth's deep core,

THORIUM

Unseen, unheard, yet forevermore,

THORIUM

It sleeps beneath the rocky ground,

THORIUM

In hidden realms where mysteries abound.

THORIUM

From ancient times, its story unfolds,

THORIUM

A tale of power, of secrets untold,

THORIUM

For eons, it lay, undisturbed,

THORIUM

A treasure trove yet to be observed.

THORIUM

But human hands, with curious minds,

THORIUM

Unveiled the power that Thorium binds,

THORIUM

In labs and reactors, its potential seen,

THORIUM

A source of energy, both clean and serene.

THORIUM

Yet Thorium's power, a double-edged blade,

THORIUM

With promises bright and shadows shade,

THORIUM

For in its heart lies nuclear might,

THORIUM

A force that could bring both day and night.

THORIUM

But heed the call of wisdom's voice,

THORIUM

For Thorium's power, we must rejoice,

THORIUM

In harnessing its might for good,

THORIUM

To fuel the world as we know we should.

THORIUM

So let us tread with cautious grace,

THORIUM

And seek the path to a brighter space,

THORIUM

Where Thorium's gift can light the way,

THORIUM

To a future where all can thrive and stay.

THORIUM

In the depths of time, Thorium's tale,

THORIUM

A story of triumph, of hope, and wail,

THORIUM

A reminder of the power we hold,

THORIUM

To shape our destiny, bold and bold.

THORIUM

In the bosom of Earth, where secrets hide,

THORIUM

Thorium slumbers, its essence tied,

THORIUM

To the rhythms of the planet's breath,

THORIUM

A silent sentinel, guarding life's breadth.

THORIUM

So let us honor this element rare,

THORIUM

With reverence, awe, and tender care,

THORIUM

For in its atoms, a universe lies,

THORIUM

A promise of tomorrow, in infinite skies.

THORIUM

ABOUT THE CREATOR

Walter the Educator is one of the pseudonyms for Walter Anderson. Formally educated in Chemistry, Business, and Education, he is an educator, an author, a diverse entrepreneur, and he is the son of a disabled war veteran. "Walter the Educator" shares his time between educating and creating. He holds interests and owns several creative projects that entertain, enlighten, enhance, and educate, hoping to inspire and motivate you.

Follow, find new works, and stay up to date with Walter the Educator™ at WaltertheEducator.com

www.ingramcontent.com/pod-product-compliance
Lightning Source LLC
LaVergne TN
LVHW010412070526
838199LV00064B/5278